I0013889

The Dify AI Playbook: Monetize AI with No-Code Chatbots & Automations

by
Silas Meadowlark

Contents

The AI Revolution is Here: Why No-Code is Your Gateway

The murmur has become a roar. Artificial intelligence, once relegated to the realm of science fiction and the heavily guarded labs of tech behemoths, is no longer a distant promise. It's here, it's now, and it's reshaping the business landscape with the force of a tidal wave. From automating tedious tasks to unlocking entirely new revenue streams, AI is poised to be the defining technology of our era. But for many, the path to harnessing its power seems daunting, shrouded in complex algorithms and requiring years of coding expertise. This is where the magic of no-code platforms like Dify comes in, offering a gateway to the AI revolution that is accessible, affordable, and empowers individuals and businesses of all sizes to participate in this transformative shift.

The AI Tsunami: Understanding the Scale of the Opportunity

Let's be clear: we are not just talking about incremental improvements. This isn't simply about faster spreadsheets or slightly more efficient workflows. AI is fundamentally altering how we interact with technology, how we make decisions, and how businesses operate. Consider the implications of AI-powered customer service that can answer inquiries 24/7 with human-like understanding, or marketing campaigns that are dynamically optimized based on real-time user behavior. Think about AI-driven product development that can identify unmet needs and predict future trends with remarkable accuracy.

The sheer scale of the opportunity is staggering. Industry analysts predict that AI will contribute trillions of dollars to the global economy in the coming years, impacting virtually every sector from healthcare and finance to manufacturing and retail. Businesses that embrace AI early and effectively will gain a significant competitive advantage, while those who remain on the sidelines risk being left behind. This is not just about staying relevant; it's about survival in a rapidly evolving marketplace. Ignoring the potential of AI is akin to ignoring the internet in the early 1990s – a decision that could prove fatal to long-term success.

But the problem, as many see it, lies in the perceived complexity. The traditional image of AI development involves armies of data scientists, machine learning engineers, and programmers wrestling with intricate code. This creates a significant barrier to entry for many businesses, particularly smaller enterprises and startups that lack the resources to invest in expensive AI infrastructure and specialized talent. The good news is that this perception is rapidly changing.

The No-Code Revolution: Democratizing AI Development

The rise of no-code platforms is fundamentally democratizing technology development. Just as drag-and-drop website builders empowered individuals to create professional-looking websites without writing a single line of HTML, no-code AI platforms are enabling anyone to build and deploy sophisticated AI applications without needing to be a coding wizard.

These platforms provide intuitive visual interfaces that allow users to build AI-powered chatbots, automate complex workflows, and analyze vast amounts of data simply by dragging and dropping pre-built components and connecting them in a logical manner. Think of it as assembling LEGO bricks – you don't need to understand the intricacies of plastic molding to build a masterpiece; you just need to know how the pieces fit together.

Dify, in particular, stands out as a powerful and versatile no-code AI platform. It offers a comprehensive suite of tools and features that allow users to build and deploy a wide range of AI applications, from simple chatbots to complex AI-driven automations, all without writing a single line of code. This accessibility is a game-changer, opening up the world of AI to a much wider audience and empowering individuals and businesses of all sizes to leverage its transformative power.

Why No-Code AI is a Game-Changer for Businesses

The benefits of adopting a no-code AI approach are numerous and far-reaching. Let's delve into some of the key advantages:

1. Increased Speed and Agility: Traditional AI development can be a slow and cumbersome process, often taking months or even years to bring a project from concept to deployment. No-code platforms dramatically accelerate this timeline, allowing businesses to rapidly prototype, test, and deploy AI applications in a matter of days or weeks. This

agility is crucial in today's fast-paced business environment, where the ability to quickly adapt and innovate is essential for staying ahead of the competition.

2. Reduced Costs: Hiring and maintaining a team of data scientists and AI engineers can be incredibly expensive. No-code platforms significantly reduce these costs by eliminating the need for specialized coding skills. This makes AI accessible to businesses with limited budgets, allowing them to compete with larger organizations on a more level playing field. Furthermore, the rapid development cycles associated with no-code platforms translate into lower overall project costs.

3. Enhanced Innovation and Experimentation: The ease of use and accessibility of no-code platforms encourage experimentation and innovation. Businesses can quickly test different AI applications and identify the most effective solutions for their specific needs. This iterative approach allows for continuous improvement and optimization, leading to better outcomes and a more data-driven decision-making process.

4. Empowered Citizen Developers: No-code platforms empower individuals within organizations who have a deep understanding of the business but lack coding skills to become "citizen developers." These individuals can use no-code tools to build AI applications that address specific pain points and improve operational efficiency. This decentralization of AI development can lead to a more agile and responsive organization.

5. Improved Customer Experience: AI-powered chatbots can provide instant and personalized customer support, improving customer satisfaction and loyalty. No-code platforms make it easy to build and deploy these chatbots, allowing businesses to provide exceptional customer service

4

24/7. Furthermore, AI can be used to personalize marketing campaigns, recommend relevant products, and create a more engaging and personalized customer experience.

Monetizing AI with Dify: Practical Examples

The possibilities for monetizing AI with Dify are virtually limitless. Here are just a few practical examples to illustrate the potential:

1. AI-Powered E-commerce Chatbots: Imagine an online store where customers can ask questions about products, track orders, and resolve issues through a sophisticated AI-powered chatbot built with Dify. This chatbot can not only provide instant answers but also personalize recommendations based on the customer's browsing history and purchase behavior, leading to increased sales and customer loyalty. The chatbot could even proactively offer discounts or promotions to customers who are about to abandon their shopping carts.

2. Automated Lead Generation and Qualification: Businesses can use Dify to build AI-powered chatbots that automatically generate and qualify leads. These chatbots can engage with website visitors, ask qualifying questions, and route promising leads to the sales team, freeing up valuable time for sales representatives to focus on closing deals. This automation can significantly improve lead generation efficiency and increase sales conversion rates.

3. Personalized Content Recommendations: Media companies and online publishers can use Dify to build AI-powered recommendation engines that personalize content recommendations for each user. These recommendation engines can analyze user behavior, preferences, and demographics to suggest articles, videos, and other content that

are most likely to be of interest. This can lead to increased engagement, longer session times, and higher advertising revenue.

4. AI-Driven Market Research: Businesses can use Dify to analyze vast amounts of data from social media, online forums, and other sources to gain insights into customer sentiment, market trends, and competitive intelligence. This AI-driven market research can help businesses make more informed decisions about product development, marketing strategy, and pricing.

5. Smart Home Automation and Control: Dify can be used to build AI-powered smart home applications that automate various tasks, such as controlling lighting, temperature, and security systems. These applications can learn user preferences and automatically adjust settings to create a more comfortable and convenient living environment.

These are just a few examples of the many ways that businesses can monetize AI with Dify. The key is to identify specific pain points and opportunities within your business and then use the platform's powerful tools and features to build AI applications that address those needs.

The Future is Now: Embracing the No-Code AI Revolution

The AI revolution is not some distant future event; it is happening right now. And with the advent of no-code platforms like Dify, the power to harness this revolution is within reach for everyone. Whether you are an entrepreneur, a small business owner, a marketer, or a developer, now is the time to embrace the potential of no-code AI and start building the future of your business. The gateway is open – are you ready to step through?

Decoding Dify: A Comprehensive Introduction

The promise of Artificial Intelligence, once relegated to the realm of science fiction, is now knocking firmly on the door of everyday business. Suddenly, tools that seemed impossibly complex are becoming accessible, thanks in no small part to platforms like Dify. But what is Dify, really? It's more than just another chatbot builder; it's a comprehensive ecosystem designed to empower you to leverage the power of AI, without requiring you to become a coding wizard. This chapter will peel back the layers of Dify, providing a detailed exploration of its core features, architecture, and the overall development workflow. By the end, you'll have a solid understanding of how Dify can be a powerful tool in your journey to monetize AI.

Understanding the Dify Philosophy: AI for Everyone

Before diving into the technical specifics, it's crucial to grasp the underlying philosophy driving Dify. The platform is fundamentally built on the idea of democratizing AI. It aims to bridge the gap between the potential of AI and the practical realities faced by entrepreneurs, small businesses, marketers, and even seasoned developers who prefer rapid prototyping and deployment.

Dify understands that not everyone has the time, resources, or inclination to delve deep into the intricacies of machine learning models, Python libraries, and complex API integrations. Instead, it provides a visual, intuitive interface that allows you to focus on the what – what you want your AI to do – rather than the how – how to code it from scratch. This "no-code" approach empowers you to rapidly experiment, iterate, and deploy AI-powered solutions, turning your ideas into tangible, revenue-generating assets.

This accessibility doesn't come at the expense of power or flexibility. Dify is designed to be scalable and customizable, allowing you to fine-tune your AI applications to meet specific needs. It offers a range of options for integrating external data sources, customizing the user interface, and controlling the behavior of the AI models. Think of it as a modular system: you can start with the building blocks provided and gradually expand and customize as your needs evolve.

Navigating the Dify User Interface: A Guided Tour

The first interaction with Dify is through its user interface, a thoughtfully designed environment that prioritizes clarity and ease of use. The layout is generally divided into several key areas, each serving a specific purpose in the AI development workflow.

The central Dashboard provides a high-level overview of your projects, including a summary of active applications, usage statistics, and recent activity. This is your home base, offering a quick snapshot of the health and performance of your AI deployments. You can quickly see which applications are consuming the most resources, identify potential bottlenecks, and track key metrics like user engagement and conversion rates.

Next comes the Application Builder, the heart of Dify. This is where you create and configure your AI applications, defining their purpose, behavior, and interaction style. The Application Builder typically features a visual canvas where you can drag and drop components, connect them to create workflows, and configure their properties. It is here that the magic truly happens. You'll define the prompts that guide the AI's responses, specify the data sources it should access, and customize the user interface to create a seamless and engaging experience.

The Dataset Management section allows you to upload, organize, and manage the data that your AI applications will use. This could include text documents, spreadsheets, images, or any other type of data that is relevant to your application's purpose. Dify provides tools for cleaning, transforming, and annotating your data, ensuring that it is in the optimal format for training and inference. This is critical, since the quality of the data directly impacts the performance of your AI models. Garbage in, garbage out, as the saying goes.

The Model Management area provides access to a range of pre-trained AI models, as well as the ability to train your own custom models. Dify supports a variety of popular model architectures, including large language models (LLMs) for text generation, image recognition models for visual tasks, and time series models for forecasting. You can choose the model that best suits your needs and fine-tune it using your own data to improve its accuracy and performance. The flexibility here is a real strength, allowing you to leverage the power of cutting-edge AI research without having to build everything from scratch.

Finally, the Deployment and Monitoring section allows you to deploy your AI applications to a variety of platforms, including web, mobile, and messaging channels. Dify provides tools for monitoring the performance of your applications in real-time, tracking key metrics like latency, error rates, and resource utilization. This allows you to identify and address any issues that may arise, ensuring that your applications are running smoothly and efficiently. Continuous monitoring is paramount for maintaining a reliable and effective AI solution.

Core Functionalities: The Building Blocks of AI Applications

Dify offers a diverse set of core functionalities that serve as the building blocks for creating sophisticated AI applications. These functionalities can be broadly categorized into several key areas:

Natural Language Processing (NLP): This is the foundation for building chatbots and other text-based AI applications. Dify provides tools for understanding and generating human language, including sentiment analysis, named entity recognition, and text summarization. You can use these tools to create chatbots that can understand user intent, extract relevant information from text, and generate intelligent responses. The power of NLP allows you to create truly conversational experiences.

Data Integration: Dify allows you to connect to a wide range of external data sources, including databases, APIs, and file systems. This allows you to integrate your AI applications with your existing business systems, enabling them to access and process real-time data. For example, you could connect your chatbot to your CRM system to provide customers with personalized support based on their past interactions. The ability to seamlessly integrate with existing data sources is crucial for building AI applications that are truly integrated into your business workflows.

Workflow Automation: Dify provides tools for automating complex tasks and processes. You can use these tools to create workflows that chain together multiple AI functionalities, such as NLP, data integration, and machine learning. For example, you could create a workflow that automatically extracts information from emails, analyzes the sentiment of the text, and then routes the email to the appropriate department. Automating these tasks can save time and resources, freeing up your team to focus on more strategic initiatives.

Machine Learning (ML): Dify allows you to train and deploy your own custom machine learning models. This allows you to create AI applications that can learn from data and make predictions or decisions based on that learning. For example, you could train a machine learning model to predict customer churn, identify fraudulent transactions, or optimize pricing strategies. The ability to leverage machine learning allows you to create AI applications that are truly intelligent and adaptive.

User Interface (UI) Customization: Dify provides a range of tools for customizing the user interface of your AI applications. This allows you to create a seamless and engaging user experience that aligns with your brand identity. You can customize the look and feel of your chatbot, add custom widgets, and integrate with other web applications. The ability to tailor the user interface is crucial for creating AI applications that are both functional and visually appealing.

The Dify Development Workflow: From Idea to Deployment

The development workflow in Dify is designed to be iterative and agile, allowing you to rapidly prototype, test, and deploy AI applications. The process typically involves the following steps:

1. Define the Use Case: The first step is to clearly define the problem you are trying to solve with AI. What are the specific goals you want to achieve? Who are your target users? What data do you need to access? A clear understanding of the use case is crucial for guiding the development process and ensuring that your AI application is aligned with your business objectives.

2. Design the Application: Once you have a clear understanding of the use case, you can begin to design the architecture of your AI application. This involves identifying the key functionalities you will need, the data sources you will need to access, and the user interface you will need to create. Dify's visual interface makes this process intuitive and straightforward.

3. Build the Application: With the design in place, you can begin to build your AI application using Dify's drag-and-drop interface and pre-built components. This involves configuring the various functionalities, connecting them to create workflows, and customizing the user interface. This is where you bring your vision to life.

4. Train and Test the Models: If your application uses machine learning, you will need to train your models using your own data. Dify provides tools for managing and annotating your data, as well as for training and evaluating your models. Thorough testing is crucial for ensuring that your models are accurate and reliable.

5. Deploy the Application: Once your application is built and tested, you can deploy it to a variety of platforms, including web, mobile, and messaging channels. Dify provides tools for managing your deployments and monitoring the performance of your applications in real-time.

6. Iterate and Improve: The development process doesn't end with deployment. You should continuously monitor the performance of your AI application, gather user feedback, and iterate on your design to improve its effectiveness. Dify's agile development workflow makes it easy to make changes and redeploy your application quickly.

Dify's Architecture: A Peek Under the Hood

While Dify abstracts away much of the underlying complexity of AI development, it's helpful to have a basic understanding of its architecture. At its core, Dify is a platform built on a modular and scalable design.

It leverages cloud-based infrastructure to provide a robust and reliable environment for running AI applications. This means you don't have to worry about managing servers or infrastructure; Dify handles all of that for you.

The platform is built on a microservices architecture, which means that it is composed of a collection of independent services that communicate with each other via APIs. This allows Dify to be highly scalable and resilient. If one service fails, the others can continue to operate normally.

Dify also incorporates a variety of open-source technologies, such as TensorFlow, PyTorch, and Kubernetes. This allows it to leverage the latest advancements in AI research and development.

The key takeaway is that Dify provides a robust and scalable platform for building and deploying AI applications, while abstracting away much of the underlying complexity. This allows you to focus on the business value of AI, rather than the technical details.

In conclusion, Dify is a comprehensive platform that democratizes AI development, making it accessible to a wider audience. By understanding its user interface, core functionalities, development workflow, and underlying architecture, you can begin to unlock the power of AI and create innovative solutions that drive business growth. The next step is to get your hands dirty and start building!

From Idea to AI App: Planning Your First Dify Project

So, you're ready to take the plunge. You've heard the whispers of AI, the promises of automation, and the potential for serious monetization. You're intrigued by Dify and its no-code approach. Fantastic. But before you dive headfirst into building your AI-powered empire, let's take a step back. Because the difference between a successful AI application and one that languishes in digital obscurity isn't magic; it's planning.

This chapter isn't about coding (thankfully, that's the point of Dify!). It's about the essential groundwork that will ensure your first Dify project isn't just a cool tech demo, but a genuine revenue-generating asset. We're talking about turning an idea into a tangible, profitable AI application.

Identifying Your AI Opportunity: Where Does the Pain Live?

The most brilliant AI in the world is useless if it doesn't solve a real problem. So, the first question you need to ask yourself isn't, "What cool AI thing can I build?" but rather, "What problem can I solve?" Think about the frustrations, inefficiencies, and bottlenecks that plague your industry, your business, or even your own daily life. These are your potential goldmines.

Think of it like this: every pain point is a potential opportunity. Are customers constantly asking the same questions on your website? Is your customer service team overwhelmed with repetitive inquiries? Are you struggling to generate leads or personalize your marketing efforts? Are there tedious, time-consuming tasks within your organization that could be automated?

Don't limit yourself to problems you already know how to solve. The beauty of AI is its ability to tackle complexities that were previously insurmountable. Consider industries ripe for disruption. Think about healthcare, education, finance, or even creative fields. Where can AI streamline processes, enhance experiences, or provide new insights?

A great way to brainstorm is to examine your own workflows and customer interactions. Put yourself in the shoes of your customers. What are their biggest frustrations? What are the things they wish were easier? Talk to your employees. What tasks do they dread? What processes slow them down?

Once you have a list of potential pain points, it's time to prioritize. Which problems are the most pressing? Which ones affect the largest number of people? Which ones are currently being poorly addressed? And, most importantly, which ones are you genuinely passionate about solving? Passion is a powerful motivator, and it will be essential when you inevitably encounter challenges along the way.

Defining Your Target Audience: Who Will Benefit?

You can't build a product for everyone. Trying to do so is a recipe for disaster. Instead, you need to identify a specific target audience – the group of people who will benefit most from your AI application. The more narrowly you define your audience, the better you can tailor your solution to their specific needs and preferences.

Consider demographics, psychographics, and behavioral patterns. What are their age, gender, location, income level, and education? What are their values, interests, and lifestyles? What are their online habits and technology preferences?

For example, if you're building an AI-powered customer service chatbot, your target audience might be small business owners who lack the resources to hire a full-time support team. Or perhaps it's e-commerce businesses that experience high volumes of customer inquiries during peak seasons.

Understanding your target audience is crucial for several reasons. First, it will inform the design and functionality of your AI application. What features will they find most valuable? What language and tone should you use? What platform will they be most likely to access it on?

Second, it will guide your marketing and sales efforts. Where do they spend their time online? What messages will resonate with them? How can you reach them most effectively?

Finally, it will help you measure the success of your application. Are you attracting the right type of users? Are they engaging with your application in the way you intended? Are they achieving the desired outcomes?

Setting Clear Goals and KPIs: How Will You Measure Success?

Before you write a single line of code (or, in Dify's case, configure a single setting), you need to define your goals and key performance indicators (KPIs). What do you hope to achieve with your AI application? How will you know if it's successful?

Your goals should be specific, measurable, achievable, relevant, and time-bound (SMART). For example, instead of saying "I want to increase sales," you might say "I want to increase sales by 10% in the next quarter using an AI-powered product recommendation engine."

Your KPIs are the metrics that you will use to track your progress towards your goals. These should be quantifiable and directly related to your desired outcomes. Some common KPIs for AI applications include:

- User engagement: How many users are interacting with your application? How often are they using it? How long are they spending on it?

- Conversion rates: How many users are completing desired actions, such as making a purchase, filling out a form, or subscribing to a newsletter?

- Customer satisfaction: How satisfied are users with your application? Are they finding it helpful and easy to use?

- Cost savings: How much money are you saving by automating tasks or improving efficiency?

- Revenue generation: How much revenue is your AI application generating?

Choosing the right KPIs is crucial for understanding whether your application is performing as expected. They will provide valuable insights into user behavior, identify areas for improvement, and help you make data-driven decisions.

Don't be afraid to adjust your goals and KPIs as you learn more about your users and your application's performance. The key is to be flexible and adaptable, and to continuously strive for improvement.

Mapping Out Your Dify Project: From Idea to Implementation

Now comes the exciting part: translating your ideas into a concrete Dify project. This involves outlining the key features and functionalities of your AI application, and determining how you will implement them within the Dify platform.

Start by creating a user flow diagram. This is a visual representation of the steps that users will take when interacting with your application. For example, if you're building a customer service chatbot, the user flow might look something like this:

1. User initiates a conversation with the chatbot.

2. Chatbot asks the user what they need help with.

3. User describes their issue.

4. Chatbot attempts to answer the user's question.

5. If the chatbot can't answer the question, it transfers the user to a human agent.

For each step in the user flow, consider the following questions:

- What information does the user need to provide?

- What information does the application need to access?

- What actions does the application need to perform?

- What is the desired outcome?

Once you have a clear understanding of the user flow, you can start mapping out the specific features and functionalities that you will need to build within Dify. This might include:

- Natural language processing (NLP): How will your application understand and interpret user input?

- Knowledge base: What information will your application need to access in order to answer user questions or perform tasks?

- Decision-making logic: How will your application make decisions based on user input and available data?

- Integration with other systems: Will your application need to connect to any external databases, APIs, or other services?

- User interface (UI): How will users interact with your application? Will it be through a chatbot, a web interface, or a mobile app?

Dify's no-code environment makes this process significantly easier. Instead of writing complex code, you can leverage Dify's pre-built components and visual interface to build your application quickly and efficiently.

Testing and Iteration: Learning from Your Users

No plan survives first contact with the enemy, as they say. Or, in this case, first contact with your users. Once you have a working prototype of your AI application, it's time to put it to the test. Gather feedback from your target audience and use it to refine your application.

Start with a small group of beta testers who are representative of your target audience. Ask them to use your application and provide honest feedback on their experience. What did they like? What did they dislike? What could be improved?

Pay close attention to how users are interacting with your application. Are they using it in the way you intended? Are they encountering any problems or frustrations? Are they achieving the desired outcomes?

Use the feedback you gather to iterate on your application. Make changes to the design, functionality, and content based on user feedback. Don't be afraid to experiment and try new things.

Testing and iteration is an ongoing process. Even after you launch your application, you should continue to gather feedback from your users and use it to improve your application over time. The AI landscape is constantly evolving, and you need to stay ahead of the curve in order to remain competitive.

The Dify Advantage: Speeding Up the Process

Dify isn't just a tool; it's an accelerator. It allows you to bypass the traditional complexities of AI development and focus on what truly matters: solving problems and creating value. Because you don't have to wrestle with intricate code, you can dedicate more time to understanding your users, refining your application, and maximizing its impact.

By leveraging Dify's no-code environment, you can significantly reduce the time and cost of developing your AI application. You can also empower non-technical team members to contribute to the development process, fostering collaboration and innovation.

Remember, the key to success with Dify is not just technical proficiency, but also a clear understanding of your target audience, your goals, and your KPIs. With a solid plan in place, you can harness the power of Dify to build a successful AI application that delivers real value to your users and generates significant revenue for your business. Now, go forth and build something amazing!

Building Your First Chatbot: A Step-by-Step Guide

So, you're ready to dive in and build your first chatbot using Dify. Fantastic! This chapter will walk you through the entire process, holding your hand every step of the way. We'll focus on creating a simple, yet functional chatbot that you can then customize and expand upon as your needs evolve. Think of this as your foundational chatbot-building block, the LEGO brick upon which you'll build your AI empire.

Defining Your Chatbot's Purpose

Before you even log into Dify, let's take a moment to clarify what exactly you want your chatbot to do. This isn't just a nice-to-have, it's absolutely critical. A chatbot without a clear purpose is like a ship without a rudder – it'll drift aimlessly and likely crash.

Ask yourself: What problem will this chatbot solve? What task will it automate? Who is the target user?

Let's imagine you run a small bakery specializing in custom cakes. A great use case for a chatbot could be handling initial order inquiries. Instead of spending hours on the phone answering the same questions – "Do you make gluten-free cakes?", "What are your pricing options?", "How far in advance do I need to order?" – your chatbot can handle these automatically, freeing you up to focus on baking those delicious masterpieces.

Therefore, our hypothetical chatbot, let's call it "Sweet-Bot," will be designed to answer frequently asked questions about your bakery, pricing, cake flavors, and ordering process. It will also collect basic information from potential customers, such as their desired cake type, date needed, and contact details.

Setting Up Your Dify Account and Project

If you haven't already, head over to the Dify website and create an account. The sign-up process is pretty straightforward. Once you're in, you'll land on the dashboard. Here's where the magic begins.

Click on the "Create New App" button. You'll be presented with a few options. Since we're building a chatbot from scratch, select "Chatbot." Give your app a descriptive name, like "SweetBot - Bakery Order Inquiries," and a brief description that outlines its purpose. This will help you keep track of your projects as you build more chatbots.

Choose a suitable AI model. Dify offers a range of models, each with its own strengths and weaknesses. For a simple FAQ-style chatbot, a general-purpose model like OpenAI's GPT-3.5 or a similar alternative should suffice. More complex chatbots requiring specialized knowledge or nuanced understanding might benefit from a more powerful model.

Designing the Conversation Flow

This is where you start mapping out the conversation your chatbot will have with users. Think of it as writing a script for a play, with the chatbot and the user as the actors. Don't worry, you don't need to be Shakespeare!

Dify provides a visual interface for designing conversation flows. You'll see a blank canvas where you can add "nodes" representing different steps in the conversation.

Start with a "Welcome" node. This is the first message your chatbot will send to the user. Keep it friendly and informative. For example:

"Hi there! Welcome to [Your Bakery Name]'s cake ordering assistant. I can answer your questions about our cakes, pricing, and ordering process. How can I help you today?"

Next, you'll need to anticipate the types of questions users might ask. Common questions for SweetBot might include:

- "What cake flavors do you offer?"

- "How much does a custom cake cost?"

- "Do you make gluten-free cakes?"

- "How far in advance do I need to order?"

For each of these questions, create a separate node. In each node, write a clear and concise answer. Remember to keep it conversational and avoid sounding too robotic.

For example, the node answering "What cake flavors do you offer?" might say:

"We offer a wide variety of cake flavors, including classic vanilla, rich chocolate, decadent red velvet, refreshing lemon, and many more! We also offer seasonal flavors and are always happy to experiment with new combinations. Do you have a particular flavor in mind?"

Now, connect the "Welcome" node to each of these question nodes. This creates the initial conversation flow.

Integrating Data Sources

While you can manually input all the information into the chatbot's nodes, it's much more efficient to integrate data sources. This allows the chatbot to dynamically retrieve information from a database, spreadsheet, or other external source.

For SweetBot, you might have a spreadsheet containing information about cake flavors, pricing, and ingredients. Dify allows you to connect to various data sources. Choose the appropriate connector and follow the instructions to link your data source to your chatbot.

Once connected, you can use variables within your chatbot's responses to dynamically insert data from your data source. For example, instead of hardcoding the list of cake flavors in the "What cake flavors do you offer?" node, you can use a variable that retrieves the list of flavors from your spreadsheet. This way, when you add or remove cake flavors from your spreadsheet, the chatbot will automatically update its responses.

This integration is a game changer, as it ensures your chatbot always has the latest information.

Training Your Chatbot with Knowledge

Even with a well-designed conversation flow and integrated data sources, your chatbot might still struggle to understand more complex or nuanced questions. This is where knowledge training comes in.

Dify allows you to upload documents, URLs, or text snippets containing information relevant to your chatbot's domain. This helps the chatbot learn about your business, products, and services.

For SweetBot, you could upload a document containing your bakery's menu, pricing information, and ordering policies. You can also provide examples of common questions and their corresponding answers.

The more knowledge you provide, the better your chatbot will be at understanding and responding to user queries. Think of it as giving your chatbot a crash course in all things related to your bakery.

Testing and Refining Your Chatbot

Once you've designed the conversation flow, integrated data sources, and trained your chatbot with knowledge, it's time to put it to the test.

Dify provides a built-in testing environment where you can interact with your chatbot as if you were a real user. Ask it different questions, try different phrasings, and see how it responds.

Pay close attention to the chatbot's responses. Are they accurate? Are they helpful? Are they conversational?

If you find any issues, don't worry! This is a normal part of the chatbot-building process. Go back and refine the conversation flow, update the data sources, or add more knowledge.

The key is to iterate and improve your chatbot over time. The more you test and refine it, the better it will become at providing a positive user experience. Consider asking friends or colleagues to test your chatbot and provide feedback. Fresh eyes can often spot issues that you might have missed.

Deploying Your Chatbot

Once you're happy with your chatbot's performance, it's time to deploy it. Dify offers several deployment options, including embedding it on your website, integrating it with messaging platforms like Facebook Messenger or WhatsApp, or using it as a standalone app.

Choose the deployment option that best suits your needs. For SweetBot, embedding it on your bakery's website would be a great way to provide customers with instant access to information and ordering assistance.

Follow the instructions provided by Dify to deploy your chatbot. Once deployed, it will be live and ready to interact with users.

Monitoring and Maintaining Your Chatbot

Deployment isn't the end of the journey. It's crucial to monitor your chatbot's performance and make ongoing improvements.

Dify provides analytics that track key metrics such as the number of conversations, user satisfaction, and common questions. Use these analytics to identify areas where your chatbot can be improved.

For example, if you notice that many users are asking the same question that your chatbot isn't answering well, you can add more knowledge or refine the conversation flow to address that question.

Regularly review your chatbot's performance and make necessary adjustments. This will ensure that it continues to provide a valuable service to your users.

Beyond the Basics: Advanced Features

Once you've mastered the basics of chatbot building, you can explore Dify's advanced features to create even more sophisticated and powerful chatbots.

Some of these features include:

- Natural Language Understanding (NLU): This allows your chatbot to better understand the intent behind user queries.

- Sentiment Analysis: This allows your chatbot to detect the emotional tone of user messages.

- Personalization: This allows your chatbot to tailor its responses to individual users.

- Integration with other tools: Dify can be integrated with other tools like CRM systems, marketing automation platforms, and payment gateways.

By leveraging these advanced features, you can create chatbots that are not only informative and helpful, but also engaging and personalized.

Building your first chatbot might seem daunting at first, but with Dify's no-code interface and this step-by-step guide, it's entirely achievable. Remember to start with a clear purpose, design a thoughtful conversation flow, integrate relevant data sources, and continuously test and refine your chatbot. Soon, you'll be amazed at the power of AI to automate tasks, improve customer service, and drive business growth. Now go forth and build! Your AI bakery assistant awaits!

Level Up: Advanced Dify Features and Integrations

So, you've mastered the basics of Dify. You've built your first chatbot, automated a few workflows, and maybe even started seeing some tangible results. Congratulations! But the journey doesn't end there. Dify is a powerful platform with a depth that allows you to create truly sophisticated AI solutions. This chapter is all about unlocking that potential, pushing the boundaries of what you thought possible with no-code AI. We're diving into advanced features and integrations that will transform your Dify projects from simple tools to revenue-generating powerhouses.

Harnessing the Power of APIs: Connecting Dify to the World

Imagine your Dify chatbot not just answering questions, but actively interacting with other services, pulling real-time data, and performing actions on your behalf. That's the power of API integrations. An API, or Application Programming Interface, is essentially a set of rules that allows different software systems to communicate with each other. In the context of Dify, this means you can connect your chatbot to virtually any service that offers an API, from CRM systems like Salesforce to e-commerce platforms like Shopify, and even social media platforms like Twitter.

Let's say you run an online clothing store. A customer asks your Dify chatbot, "Do you have any blue shirts in size medium that are in stock?" Without API integration, your chatbot might be limited to generic answers based on pre-programmed knowledge. But with a Shopify API integration, the chatbot can directly query your store's inventory in real-time. It can then respond with a definitive "Yes, we have three blue shirts in size medium currently in stock. They are the 'Ocean Breeze Tee,' the 'Azure Polo,' and the 'Midnight Denim Shirt.' Would you like to see details for any of these?"

That's a dramatically improved customer experience. It's instant, accurate, and personalized. And it's all powered by the seamless integration of Dify with an external API.

The specific steps for integrating an API will vary depending on the API itself. However, Dify typically provides a user-friendly interface where you can input the necessary API keys, endpoints, and request parameters. You'll likely need to consult the API documentation for the service you're connecting to in order to understand how to format your requests and interpret the responses. Don't be intimidated by the technical jargon. Most APIs have well-documented examples that you can adapt for your specific needs.

Think about some other potential use cases:

- Real Estate: Integrate with a local MLS (Multiple Listing Service) API to provide up-to-date property listings to potential buyers.

- Travel Agency: Connect to flight and hotel booking APIs to allow users to search for and book travel arrangements directly through your chatbot.

- Financial Services: Integrate with stock market APIs to provide real-time stock quotes and market analysis.

The possibilities are truly endless. The key is to identify the services that are relevant to your business and explore their API offerings. With a little bit of effort, you can transform your Dify chatbot into a powerful, data-driven tool.

Unleashing Custom Code: When No-Code Needs a Little Help

Dify's no-code interface is incredibly powerful, but there are times when you might need to venture beyond its built-in capabilities. Perhaps you need to perform a complex calculation, manipulate data in a specific way, or interact with a service that doesn't have a readily available API. That's where custom code snippets come in.

Dify allows you to inject small pieces of code, typically written in Python, directly into your workflows. This gives you the flexibility to handle tasks that would be difficult or impossible to achieve with the no-code interface alone.

For example, imagine you're building a chatbot that helps users calculate their Body Mass Index (BMI). While you could potentially achieve this with a series of conditional statements and calculations within Dify's visual editor, it would be much cleaner and more efficient to use a custom code snippet.

You could write a simple Python function that takes the user's height and weight as input, calculates the BMI, and returns the result. This function can then be easily integrated into your Dify workflow, allowing you to provide a quick and accurate BMI calculation to your users.

The beauty of custom code snippets is that they allow you to leverage the power of programming without having to build an entire application from scratch. You can use them to augment Dify's existing functionality and create highly customized solutions.

However, a word of caution: while custom code snippets can be incredibly powerful, they also introduce the potential for errors. It's important to test your code thoroughly and ensure that it's properly integrated into your Dify workflow. If you're not comfortable writing code yourself, consider working with a developer to create the necessary snippets.

Advanced Data Analysis: Turning Information into Insights

Your Dify chatbots are constantly collecting data: user questions, responses, feedback, and more. This data is a goldmine of insights that can help you improve your chatbot's performance, optimize your business processes, and make better decisions.

Dify provides built-in analytics dashboards that give you a high-level overview of your chatbot's performance. You can track metrics such as the number of conversations, the average conversation length, and the most frequently asked questions.

But to truly unlock the power of this data, you need to go beyond the basic dashboards. You need to perform advanced data analysis to identify trends, patterns, and anomalies that might otherwise go unnoticed.

One way to do this is to export your Dify data to a separate data analysis tool, such as Google Sheets, Excel, or a dedicated business intelligence platform like Tableau or Power BI. These tools provide a wide range of features for data visualization, statistical analysis, and reporting.

For example, you could use sentiment analysis techniques to analyze the tone of user messages and identify areas where your chatbot is failing to meet user expectations. You could use cluster analysis to group users based on their behavior and tailor your chatbot's responses to specific user segments. You could use regression analysis to identify the factors that are most strongly correlated with user satisfaction or conversion rates.

The key is to ask the right questions and then use data analysis techniques to find the answers. Don't be afraid to experiment with different methods and tools. The more you explore your data, the more insights you'll uncover.

Moreover, consider integrating Dify with data warehousing solutions like Google BigQuery or Amazon Redshift. This allows you to store and analyze large volumes of data from multiple sources, providing a comprehensive view of your business.

Orchestrating Complex Workflows: Building AI-Powered Automations

At this point, you're probably starting to see how Dify can be used to create more than just simple chatbots. It can be used to build complex, AI-powered automations that streamline your business processes and improve your efficiency.

Imagine a scenario where a customer submits a support request through your Dify chatbot. Instead of simply logging the request and waiting for a human agent to respond, the chatbot can automatically analyze the request, identify the relevant issue, and route it to the appropriate team. It can even suggest potential solutions based on its knowledge base and previous interactions.

This is just one example of how Dify can be used to orchestrate complex workflows. Other potential use cases include:

- Lead Generation: Automatically qualify leads based on their responses to chatbot questions and route them to the sales team.

- Order Processing: Automate the entire order processing workflow, from order placement to payment processing to shipping.

- Customer Onboarding: Guide new customers through the onboarding process with personalized instructions and support.

The key to building successful AI-powered automations is to carefully map out your existing workflows and identify areas where Dify can add value. Think about the tasks that are repetitive, time-consuming, or prone to error. These are the tasks that are most likely to benefit from automation.

Once you've identified the target processes, you can use Dify's visual editor to design workflows that automate these tasks. Be sure to test your workflows thoroughly and iterate as needed to ensure that they are performing as expected.

The Monetization Mindset: Turning Advanced Features into Revenue Streams

Ultimately, the goal of leveraging these advanced Dify features is to drive revenue. It's about transforming your Dify projects from cost centers into profit centers.

Consider these monetization strategies:

- Premium Chatbot Subscriptions: Offer advanced features, such as API integrations or custom code snippets, as part of a premium subscription package.

- Consulting Services: Help other businesses build and deploy sophisticated Dify solutions.

- Affiliate Marketing: Integrate affiliate links into your chatbot's responses and earn commissions on sales.

- Lead Generation: Generate leads for other businesses and charge them a fee for each lead.

The key is to think creatively and identify ways to leverage your Dify skills and expertise to create value for others. The more value you provide, the more revenue you'll generate.

By mastering these advanced Dify features and embracing a monetization mindset, you can unlock the full potential of the platform and create a thriving AI-powered business. The future of AI is no-code, and Dify is your key to unlocking that future. Now go out there and build something amazing!

Monetization Strategies: Turning AI into Revenue

The siren song of artificial intelligence has lured many a hopeful entrepreneur, promising efficiency, insight, and ultimately, profit. But transforming a clever AI application into a sustainable revenue stream requires more than just technical prowess; it demands a well-defined monetization strategy. With Dify, even those without coding expertise can build powerful AI tools. This chapter will explore the diverse landscape of monetization models available for your Dify-powered creations, moving beyond the theoretical and into the practical with real-world examples and case studies. We'll dissect the nuances of each approach, empowering you to choose the strategy that best aligns with your application's capabilities and your target audience's needs.

Subscription Models: Building Recurring Revenue

The subscription model, a mainstay of the modern digital economy, offers a predictable and recurring revenue stream. It's a simple concept: users pay a recurring fee (monthly, quarterly, or annually) in exchange for access to your AI application's features and benefits. The key to a successful subscription model lies in providing consistent value and continuously improving the user experience.

Consider a Dify-based AI writing assistant aimed at bloggers and content creators. Instead of charging a one-time fee, you could offer different subscription tiers: "Basic" for generating short-form content and basic SEO optimization, "Pro" for longer articles, keyword research, and plagiarism checking, and "Enterprise" for team collaboration, advanced analytics, and dedicated support. Each tier unlocks progressively more powerful features, catering to different user segments and their varying needs.

The beauty of this approach is its scalability. As your user base grows, your recurring revenue expands proportionally. Furthermore, it allows you to invest in continuous development and improvement, ensuring that your AI assistant remains competitive and valuable.

However, subscriptions aren't a one-size-fits-all solution. To make it work, you need to demonstrate clear and ongoing value. What problems does your AI solve, and how effectively does it do so? Consider offering a free trial or a freemium version with limited functionality to allow potential subscribers to experience the benefits firsthand. Gather user feedback religiously and use it to refine your application and subscription tiers.

Churn, the rate at which subscribers cancel their subscriptions, is the nemesis of any subscription-based business. To combat churn, focus on customer satisfaction. Provide excellent support, proactively address user concerns, and consistently deliver new features and improvements. Think about implementing a loyalty program to reward long-term subscribers and incentivize them to stay.

A compelling example of a successful subscription model in the AI space is Grammarly. While they offer a free version, their premium subscription unlocks advanced grammar and style checks, plagiarism detection, and vocabulary enhancement suggestions, making it an indispensable tool for writers and editors worldwide. They consistently update their AI engine and add new features, justifying the recurring cost for their subscribers.

Usage-Based Pricing: Pay-as-You-Go AI

Also known as "pay-as-you-go" pricing, usage-based pricing aligns costs directly with the consumption of your AI application's resources. This model is particularly well-suited for applications that have variable usage patterns or that offer computationally intensive features. It's fair to users who only need the AI occasionally while allowing you to capture more revenue from heavy users.

Imagine a Dify-powered AI image upscaler. Instead of charging a flat subscription fee, you could charge users based on the number of images they upscale or the resolution of the upscaled images. This way, a casual user who only upscales a few photos a month pays a minimal amount, while a professional photographer who upscales hundreds of images pays accordingly.

The key to successful usage-based pricing is transparency and predictability. Users need to understand how their usage translates into costs. Provide clear pricing tiers and usage dashboards that allow them to monitor their consumption and avoid unexpected charges.

This model is particularly effective when your AI application relies on expensive infrastructure, such as powerful GPUs for image processing or large language models for text generation. By charging based on usage, you can ensure that you're covering your costs and maintaining a healthy profit margin.

A good example is OpenAI's API pricing for their GPT models. Developers pay based on the number of tokens (words or parts of words) processed by the AI. This allows them to build a wide range of applications, from chatbots to content generators, and only pay for the AI resources they actually consume. This flexible pricing has been a key factor in the widespread adoption of OpenAI's technology.

However, usage-based pricing can be challenging to implement effectively. You need to carefully analyze your application's resource consumption and set prices that are both competitive and profitable. You also need to provide excellent support to users who may have questions about their usage and billing.

Lead Generation: AI as a Gateway to Sales

Lead generation is a powerful monetization strategy where your Dify-based AI application acts as a tool to attract potential customers for other products or services. The AI application itself might be free or offered at a low cost, with the primary goal of capturing leads and nurturing them into paying customers.

Consider a Dify-powered AI chatbot designed to help small businesses create marketing plans. The chatbot could offer a free initial consultation, providing personalized recommendations and insights based on the business's specific needs. At the end of the consultation, the chatbot could offer the option to purchase a more comprehensive marketing plan or to connect with a marketing consultant for further assistance.

The key to successful lead generation is to provide genuine value to the user upfront. The AI application should be helpful and informative, building trust and establishing your expertise. The transition from free tool to paid product or service should be seamless and natural, offering a clear and compelling reason for the user to upgrade.

This strategy works particularly well for businesses that

offer complex or customized products or services. The AI application can help to qualify leads, identify their needs, and tailor the sales pitch accordingly.

A real-world example is mortgage comparison websites that use AI-powered tools to analyze a user's financial situation and recommend suitable mortgage options. The website itself might be free to use, but the company earns revenue by connecting users with mortgage lenders and earning a commission on successful loan applications. The AI acts as a lead generation engine, driving qualified leads to the lenders.

However, lead generation requires a strong sales and marketing infrastructure. You need to have a well-defined process for nurturing leads and converting them into paying customers. You also need to be careful to comply with privacy regulations and ensure that you're not spamming users with unwanted marketing messages.

Affiliate Marketing: Earning Commissions Through Recommendations

Affiliate marketing involves promoting other companies' products or services and earning a commission on sales generated through your unique affiliate link. Your Dify-based AI application can be used to recommend relevant products or services to users, earning you a commission on each successful referral.

Imagine a Dify-powered AI chatbot that helps users find the best travel deals. The chatbot could integrate with various travel booking platforms and recommend hotels, flights, and activities based on the user's preferences and budget. Each time a user books a trip through the chatbot's affiliate link, you earn a commission from the travel booking platform.

The key to successful affiliate marketing is relevance and trust. The products or services you recommend should be genuinely helpful and relevant to your users' needs. You should also be transparent about your affiliate relationships, disclosing that you earn a commission on sales generated through your links.

This strategy works particularly well for applications that provide personalized recommendations or that cater to a specific niche. The AI can analyze user data and identify the products or services that are most likely to be of interest to them.

Amazon Associates is a classic example of an affiliate marketing program. Bloggers and website owners can earn commissions by recommending products on Amazon. A Dify-powered AI chatbot could be used to recommend products based on user queries, earning the chatbot owner a commission on each sale.

However, affiliate marketing requires careful selection of affiliate programs and a focus on providing value to users. You need to choose affiliate programs that offer competitive commissions and that align with your brand's values. You also need to be careful not to overwhelm users with too many recommendations or to promote products that are of low quality.

Choosing the Right Monetization Strategy

The optimal monetization strategy for your Dify-based AI application depends on a variety of factors, including the application's features, target audience, and competitive landscape. There's no universal solution; you'll need to carefully evaluate your options and experiment to find what works best for you.

Consider these questions when making your decision:

- What value does your AI application provide? How does it solve a problem or fulfill a need for your target audience?

- Who is your target audience? What are their needs, preferences, and willingness to pay?

- What are your costs? How much does it cost to develop, maintain, and support your AI application?

- What are your competitors doing? What monetization strategies are they using, and how successful are they?

Don't be afraid to experiment with different monetization models and to iterate based on user feedback and market data. You might even consider combining multiple monetization strategies to maximize your revenue potential. For example, you could offer a freemium version of your application to attract users, and then upsell them to a paid subscription for advanced features. Or you could use your AI application to generate leads for other products or services, while also earning commissions through affiliate marketing.

The key is to be adaptable and to continuously refine your monetization strategy as your business evolves. The world of AI is constantly changing, and you need to be prepared to adapt your approach to stay ahead of the curve.

By carefully considering your options and implementing a well-defined monetization strategy, you can transform your Dify-based AI application from a promising project into a sustainable and profitable business. The possibilities are vast, and the potential rewards are significant. Now, go forth and monetize!

Marketing Your AI App: Reaching Your Target Audience

So, you've poured your heart and soul (and perhaps a few late nights fueled by lukewarm coffee) into building an amazing AI application using Dify. It's slick, it's smart, and it solves a real problem. Congratulations! But here's the thing: even the most brilliant AI is useless if nobody knows it exists. That's where marketing comes in.

This chapter isn't about flashy gimmicks or overnight success. It's about building a sustainable strategy to connect your AI app with the people who will truly benefit from it. We're talking about finding your tribe, the folks who are actively searching for a solution like yours, and showing them why your AI app is the answer.

Understanding Your Ideal Customer

Before you even think about crafting a single social media post or writing a line of ad copy, you need a crystal-clear picture of your ideal customer. This isn't just about demographics; it's about understanding their pain points, their aspirations, and where they spend their time online. Think of it as creating a detailed avatar, a representative of the person most likely to become a loyal user of your AI app.

Ask yourself questions like: What problems are they facing in their daily lives or business? What are they currently doing to solve those problems? What are the limitations of those existing solutions? What are their goals and ambitions? Where do they go to find information and advice? What social media platforms are they most active on? What kind of content do they engage with? Are they tech-savvy, or do they prefer a more user-friendly approach?

The more specific you can be, the better. Instead of saying "small business owners," think about "solopreneurs in the e-commerce space struggling with customer service overload." Instead of "marketers," think about "digital marketing managers at startups who are overwhelmed by the sheer volume of data they need to analyze."

This detailed understanding will inform every aspect of your marketing strategy, from the keywords you target in your SEO efforts to the tone and style of your social media posts. It will ensure that your marketing efforts are laser-focused on the people who are most likely to convert into paying customers.

Laying the Foundation: Search Engine Optimization (SEO)

In today's digital landscape, SEO is the bedrock of any successful online marketing strategy. It's the process of optimizing your website and content to rank higher in search engine results pages (SERPs), so that when people search for solutions related to your AI app, they find you.

Forget the old-school tricks of keyword stuffing and spammy backlinks. Modern SEO is about providing valuable, relevant content that answers people's questions and solves their problems. It's about building a website that's user-friendly, mobile-responsive, and technically sound.

Start with keyword research. Use tools like Google Keyword Planner, Ahrefs, or SEMrush to identify the keywords and phrases that your ideal customers are using to search for solutions like yours. Focus on long-tail keywords – longer, more specific phrases that indicate a higher level of intent. For example, instead of targeting the keyword "chatbot," try targeting "AI chatbot for e-commerce customer service."

Once you've identified your target keywords, weave them naturally into your website copy, blog posts, and other content. Optimize your website's meta descriptions and title tags to entice people to click through from the search results. Make sure your website is mobile-friendly and loads quickly, as these are important ranking factors.

Don't underestimate the power of building high-quality backlinks from reputable websites. This signals to search engines that your website is a trusted source of information. You can earn backlinks by creating valuable content that others will want to link to, by guest blogging on relevant websites, or by participating in industry forums and communities.

SEO is a long-term game. It takes time and effort to build authority and climb the search engine rankings. But the results are well worth it. By investing in SEO, you can attract a steady stream of qualified leads to your AI app, without having to rely solely on paid advertising.

Social Media Marketing: Building a Community

Social media is a powerful tool for building brand awareness, connecting with your target audience, and driving traffic to your AI app. But it's not about broadcasting your message to the masses. It's about engaging in meaningful conversations, providing value, and building a community around your brand.

Choose your platforms wisely. Don't try to be everywhere at once. Focus on the platforms where your ideal customers are most active. If you're targeting B2B customers, LinkedIn is a natural choice. If you're targeting a younger audience, TikTok or Instagram might be more effective.

Create content that resonates with your audience. Share tips, insights, and tutorials related to your AI app. Answer questions, respond to comments, and participate in relevant discussions. Run contests and giveaways to generate excitement and engagement.

Don't be afraid to show your personality. People connect with brands that are authentic and relatable. Share behind-the-scenes glimpses of your company culture, your team, and the challenges you're facing.

Social media is a two-way street. It's not just about promoting your AI app; it's about listening to your audience and understanding their needs. Use social media to gather feedback, identify pain points, and improve your product.

Content Marketing: Providing Value and Building Authority

Content marketing is the process of creating and distributing valuable, relevant, and consistent content to attract and engage your target audience. It's about providing value upfront, building trust, and positioning yourself as an expert in your field.

Think beyond just writing blog posts. Consider creating ebooks, white papers, infographics, videos, and podcasts. The key is to create content that is informative, engaging, and tailored to the needs of your ideal customer.

For example, if your AI app helps businesses automate their marketing tasks, you could create a series of blog posts on topics like "5 Ways AI Can Improve Your Email Marketing," "How to Use AI to Generate More Leads," or "The Ultimate Guide to AI-Powered Content Creation."

You could also create a white paper on the benefits of AI-powered marketing automation, or a video tutorial on how to use your AI app to streamline your marketing workflows.

Promote your content through social media, email marketing, and other channels. Encourage your audience to share your content with their networks. Track your results and analyze what's working and what's not.

Content marketing is a long-term strategy. It takes time to build a library of valuable content and establish yourself as an authority in your field. But the results are well worth it. By consistently providing value to your audience, you can attract more leads, build stronger relationships, and drive more sales of your AI app.

Paid Advertising: Amplifying Your Reach

Paid advertising can be a powerful way to amplify your reach and drive targeted traffic to your AI app. But it's important to approach it strategically and avoid wasting money on ineffective campaigns.

Start by defining your goals. What do you want to achieve with your paid advertising campaigns? Do you want to generate leads, drive sales, or increase brand awareness?

Choose your platforms wisely. Google Ads is a great option for reaching people who are actively searching for solutions like yours. Social media advertising platforms like Facebook, Instagram, and LinkedIn allow you to target specific demographics and interests.

Craft compelling ad copy that speaks directly to the needs of your target audience. Use strong calls to action that encourage people to click through to your website.

Test different ad variations to see what works best. Experiment with different headlines, images, and calls to action. Track your results and optimize your campaigns based on the data.

Don't be afraid to invest in retargeting. Retargeting allows you to show ads to people who have previously visited your website but haven't yet converted. This can be a highly effective way to nudge them closer to becoming a customer.

Paid advertising can be expensive, so it's important to track your ROI (return on investment) and make sure you're getting a good return for your money. Don't be afraid to adjust your campaigns or try new strategies if you're not seeing the results you want.

Measuring Your Success

Marketing isn't a "set it and forget it" activity. It's an ongoing process of experimentation, analysis, and optimization. To ensure that your marketing efforts are paying off, you need to track your results and measure your success.

Use analytics tools like Google Analytics to track website traffic, engagement, and conversions. Monitor your social media metrics to see how your content is performing and how your audience is engaging with your brand.

Track your lead generation efforts to see how many leads you're generating from each marketing channel. Analyze your sales data to see which marketing channels are driving the most sales.

Use this data to identify what's working and what's not. Optimize your marketing campaigns based on the data. Experiment with new strategies and tactics.

The key is to be data-driven and constantly iterate on

your marketing strategy. By continuously measuring your results and making adjustments as needed, you can ensure that your marketing efforts are as effective as possible.

Marketing your AI app is an ongoing journey, not a destination. By understanding your target audience, laying a solid foundation with SEO, building a community on social media, providing value with content marketing, amplifying your reach with paid advertising, and measuring your success, you can connect your amazing AI app with the people who need it most and ultimately drive sustainable business growth. Remember, patience and persistence are key. Keep learning, keep experimenting, and keep providing value to your audience, and you'll be well on your way to success.

Scaling Your AI Business: Growth and Optimization

So, you've built your AI-powered business, maybe a nifty chatbot helping restaurants manage reservations, or an automated system crafting personalized marketing emails. You're seeing traction, users are happy, and the revenue stream is trickling... beautifully. But the trickle needs to become a torrent. You're ready to scale. But scaling isn't just about doing more of what you're already doing. It's about building a robust, efficient, and adaptable system that can handle exponential growth without collapsing under its own weight. This chapter delves into the crucial aspects of scaling your AI business, ensuring you not only survive but thrive in the dynamic landscape of artificial intelligence.

Infrastructure Optimization: Building a Solid Foundation

Think of your infrastructure as the foundation of a skyscraper. A flimsy base might hold a small house, but it'll crumble under the pressure of a towering structure. Similarly, your initial infrastructure setup, perfectly adequate for a handful of users, might buckle when faced with hundreds or thousands. This is where infrastructure optimization comes into play. It's about ensuring your systems can handle the increased load, maintain performance, and remain cost-effective as your business grows.

One of the first things to consider is your hosting environment. Shared hosting, while affordable for initial development, quickly becomes a bottleneck as your user base expands. Cloud-based solutions like AWS, Google Cloud, or Azure offer the scalability and flexibility you need. They allow you to dynamically allocate resources based on demand, meaning you only pay for what you use. This is especially crucial for AI applications, which can be resource-intensive.

Beyond raw computing power, you need to optimize the way your AI models are deployed and served. Consider using containerization technologies like Docker and orchestration platforms like Kubernetes. These tools allow you to package your AI applications into portable containers, making them easy to deploy and manage across different environments. Kubernetes, in particular, automates the deployment, scaling, and management of containerized applications, ensuring high availability and resilience.

Another critical aspect is data storage and management. As your business grows, the amount of data you generate will explode. You need a robust system to store, process, and analyze this data efficiently. Cloud-based data warehouses like Snowflake or BigQuery offer scalable and cost-effective solutions for storing and analyzing large datasets. Consider implementing data pipelines to automate the flow of data from various sources to your data warehouse, ensuring data quality and consistency.

Furthermore, pay close attention to your API infrastructure. Your AI applications likely expose APIs for other applications or services to interact with. Optimizing your API infrastructure is crucial for ensuring responsiveness and reliability. Consider using API gateways to manage and secure your APIs. API gateways can handle tasks like authentication, authorization, rate limiting, and traffic management, freeing up your AI applications to focus on processing requests. Caching frequently accessed data can also significantly improve API performance.

Finally, don't underestimate the importance of monitoring and logging. Implement robust monitoring systems to track the performance of your infrastructure and applications. Use tools like Prometheus and Grafana to visualize key metrics and identify potential bottlenecks. Logging is also crucial for debugging and troubleshooting issues. Centralized logging systems like ELK stack (Elasticsearch, Logstash, Kibana) can help you collect, analyze, and visualize logs from various sources, making it easier to identify and resolve problems.

Team Building: Assembling Your A-Team

Scaling your AI business isn't just about technology; it's also about people. You need to build a talented and dedicated team to support your growth. But finding the right people, especially in the competitive AI landscape, can be challenging.

Start by defining the roles you need to fill. Consider your current needs and future growth plans. Do you need more developers to build new features? Data scientists to improve your AI models? Customer support agents to handle increasing inquiries? Be specific about the skills and experience required for each role.

When recruiting, don't just focus on technical skills. Look for candidates with a strong problem-solving ability, a willingness to learn, and a passion for AI. Cultural fit is also crucial. You want to build a team that is collaborative, supportive, and aligned with your company's values.

Consider offering competitive salaries and benefits to attract top talent. Also, highlight the exciting opportunities that your company offers, such as the chance to work on cutting-edge AI projects, learn new skills, and make a real impact.

Once you've hired your team, invest in their training and development. Provide them with opportunities to learn new technologies, attend conferences, and participate in online courses. Encourage them to experiment with new ideas and contribute to the company's knowledge base.

Effective communication is essential for team success. Establish clear communication channels and processes. Use tools like Slack or Microsoft Teams to facilitate communication and collaboration. Hold regular team meetings to discuss progress, share ideas, and address challenges.

Delegate responsibilities effectively. Empower your team members to take ownership of their work and make decisions. Provide them with the resources and support they need to succeed.

Finally, foster a positive and supportive work environment. Recognize and reward employees for their contributions. Celebrate successes and learn from failures. Create a culture of innovation and continuous improvement.

Customer Support: Keeping Customers Happy at Scale

As your user base grows, so will the volume of customer inquiries. Providing excellent customer support is crucial for retaining customers and building a strong brand reputation. But scaling customer support can be challenging, especially with limited resources.

One of the first things to consider is automating common support tasks. Chatbots, powered by AI, can handle routine inquiries, answer frequently asked questions, and provide basic troubleshooting. This frees up your human support agents to focus on more complex issues.

Consider implementing a knowledge base or FAQ section on your website. This allows customers to find answers to common questions without having to contact support. Make sure your knowledge base is well-organized, easy to navigate, and regularly updated.

When customers do need to contact support, make it easy for them to do so. Offer multiple channels of communication, such as email, phone, and live chat. Ensure that your support agents are well-trained, knowledgeable, and empathetic.

Implement a ticketing system to track and manage customer inquiries. This ensures that no inquiry falls through the cracks and that each customer receives a timely response. Use analytics to track key metrics such as response time, resolution time, and customer satisfaction.

Proactive support can also be a powerful way to improve customer satisfaction. Consider reaching out to customers who are experiencing difficulties or who haven't used your product in a while. Offer them assistance and guidance.

Finally, solicit feedback from your customers on a regular basis. Use surveys, feedback forms, and social media monitoring to gather insights into their experiences. Use this feedback to improve your product and your support processes.

Ongoing Product Development: Staying Ahead of the Curve

The AI landscape is constantly evolving. New technologies emerge, user expectations change, and competitors release new products. To stay ahead of the curve, you need to continuously develop and improve your AI products.

One of the most important things is to listen to your customers. Gather feedback on what they like and dislike about your product. Identify pain points and areas for improvement. Use this feedback to inform your product roadmap.

Keep a close eye on your competitors. See what they're doing well and where they're falling short. Identify opportunities to differentiate your product and offer unique value.

Experiment with new technologies and approaches. Don't be afraid to try new things. Conduct A/B tests to see what works best. Continuously iterate and improve your product based on the results of your experiments.

Invest in research and development. Explore new AI techniques and algorithms. Stay up-to-date on the latest advancements in the field. Consider partnering with universities or research institutions to access cutting-edge research.

Regularly release new features and updates. This shows your customers that you're committed to improving your product and that you're responsive to their needs.

Don't forget about maintenance and bug fixes. Regularly check your product for bugs and security vulnerabilities. Address them promptly.

Finally, plan for the future. Think about where you want your product to be in one year, five years, or even ten years. Develop a long-term product roadmap that outlines your vision and strategy.

Scaling an AI business is a marathon, not a sprint. It requires careful planning, execution, and continuous optimization. By focusing on infrastructure, team building, customer support, and product development, you can build a sustainable and thriving AI business that delivers value to your customers and generates long-term revenue. Remember, the beauty of no-code is that it allows you to iterate and adapt rapidly, so embrace the change and keep learning! The future of AI is bright, and with the right approach, your business can be a shining star.

Real-World Success Stories: Dify in Action

The beauty of Dify lies not just in its technical capabilities, but in its transformative power when applied to real-world business challenges. Theory is important, but witnessing concrete examples of success is what truly ignites the imagination and provides a roadmap for your own AI-powered journey. This chapter dives deep into several compelling case studies across diverse industries, showcasing how Dify has been instrumental in driving revenue, streamlining operations, and enhancing customer experiences. We'll explore the specific problems these businesses faced, the Dify solutions they implemented, and the tangible results they achieved. Get ready to be inspired and discover the untapped potential of AI within your own organization.

Personalized Learning Revolution: Elevating Educational Experiences with Dify

Imagine a world where every student has access to a personalized tutor, available 24/7, tailored to their individual learning style and pace. That's the vision that "EduSpark," an innovative online education platform, is bringing to life using Dify. EduSpark offers a wide range of courses, from basic math to advanced programming, and they were struggling to provide adequate support to their rapidly growing student base. Traditional methods like email and forum support were proving insufficient, leading to student frustration and high churn rates.

The team at EduSpark recognized the need for a scalable and personalized solution. They envisioned an AI-powered learning assistant that could answer student questions, provide personalized feedback, and even offer encouragement during challenging moments. After evaluating several options, they chose Dify for its ease of use, flexibility, and robust API capabilities.

Their Dify-powered solution, affectionately named "Athena," is integrated directly into the EduSpark platform. Students can access Athena through a chat interface, posing questions related to course content, assignments, or even general study tips. Athena leverages a vast knowledge base built from EduSpark's course materials, FAQs, and expert insights. But the real magic lies in its ability to personalize the learning experience.

Using Dify's advanced natural language processing (NLP) capabilities, Athena analyzes each student's question to understand their specific needs and learning style. For example, if a student is struggling with a particular math concept, Athena might offer a simplified explanation, provide additional examples, or even suggest alternative learning resources. If a student is feeling discouraged, Athena might offer words of encouragement and remind them of their progress.

The results have been nothing short of remarkable. EduSpark has seen a significant decrease in student churn, with students reporting higher levels of satisfaction and engagement. The platform has also witnessed a dramatic reduction in the workload of its human tutors, freeing them up to focus on more complex and individualized student needs.

One of the most impactful features of Athena is its ability to provide instant feedback on practice exercises. Students can submit their answers directly to Athena, which then analyzes their work and provides detailed feedback, highlighting areas of strength and areas for improvement. This instant feedback loop has proven to be incredibly effective in helping students master new concepts and build confidence.

EduSpark is now exploring new ways to leverage Dify to further personalize the learning experience. They are experimenting with using Athena to create personalized learning pathways for each student, tailoring the curriculum to their individual needs and goals. They are also exploring the possibility of using Athena to provide real-time assessment of student understanding, allowing instructors to adjust their teaching methods on the fly. EduSpark's story is a testament to the power of AI to transform education and empower students to achieve their full potential.

Revolutionizing E-commerce Customer Service: Streamlining Support and Boosting Sales at "Style Haven"

In the fast-paced world of e-commerce, providing exceptional customer service is paramount to success. "Style Haven," a popular online fashion retailer, understood this all too well. They were experiencing a surge in customer inquiries, overwhelming their support team and leading to long response times and frustrated customers. Common inquiries ranged from order tracking and product availability to sizing questions and return policies.

Style Haven needed a solution that could handle the high volume of customer inquiries efficiently and effectively, without sacrificing the personalized touch that their customers valued. They turned to Dify to build an AI-powered virtual assistant that could provide instant support and guidance to their customers, 24/7.

Their Dify-powered virtual assistant, named "Stella," is integrated directly into the Style Haven website and mobile app. Customers can access Stella through a chat interface, asking questions in natural language. Stella is trained on a comprehensive knowledge base of Style Haven's products, policies, and FAQs, allowing her to answer a wide range of customer inquiries accurately and efficiently.

One of the key features of Stella is her ability to handle order tracking inquiries. Customers can simply ask Stella about the status of their order, and she will provide them with real-time updates, including tracking information and estimated delivery dates. This feature has significantly reduced the number of order-related inquiries handled by the human support team, freeing them up to focus on more complex issues.

Stella is also adept at answering product-related questions. Customers can ask Stella about the materials used in a particular garment, the available sizes, or even styling tips. Stella leverages Style Haven's product catalog and image database to provide detailed and accurate information to customers.

But Stella's capabilities extend beyond simply answering questions. She can also proactively offer assistance to customers, such as suggesting related products or providing personalized styling recommendations. For example, if a customer is browsing a particular dress, Stella might suggest complementary accessories or other dresses in a similar style. This proactive approach has helped Style Haven increase sales and improve customer engagement.

The results of implementing Stella have been impressive. Style Haven has seen a significant reduction in customer service costs, with Stella handling a large percentage of customer inquiries. They have also seen a marked improvement in customer satisfaction, with customers reporting shorter response times and more helpful support. Furthermore, Stella has contributed to an increase in sales by proactively offering product recommendations and personalized styling advice. Style Haven's success story demonstrates the power of Dify to transform e-commerce customer service and drive business growth.

Streamlining Healthcare Administration: Improving Efficiency and Patient Experience at "CareWell Clinic"

The healthcare industry is often burdened by complex administrative processes, leading to inefficiencies and frustrated patients. "CareWell Clinic," a large multi-specialty clinic, recognized the need to streamline their administrative operations and improve the overall patient experience. They were struggling with a high volume of phone calls, long wait times for appointments, and difficulty managing patient records.

CareWell Clinic decided to leverage Dify to build an AI-powered virtual assistant that could automate many of their administrative tasks and provide patients with instant access to information and support.

Their Dify-powered virtual assistant, named "WellBot," is integrated into the CareWell Clinic website and mobile app. Patients can access WellBot through a chat interface, asking questions about appointment scheduling, medication refills, insurance coverage, and other common inquiries.

One of the most impactful features of WellBot is its ability to handle appointment scheduling. Patients can use WellBot to book appointments with their preferred doctor, at a time that is convenient for them. WellBot integrates with CareWell Clinic's scheduling system to ensure that appointments are booked accurately and efficiently. This feature has significantly reduced the number of phone calls handled by the reception staff and has made it easier for patients to schedule appointments.

WellBot is also capable of handling medication refill requests. Patients can use WellBot to request refills of their prescriptions, and WellBot will automatically submit the request to the appropriate pharmacy. This feature has saved patients time and effort and has reduced the risk of medication errors.

In addition to handling appointment scheduling and medication refills, WellBot can also answer common questions about insurance coverage, billing inquiries, and other administrative matters. WellBot is trained on a comprehensive knowledge base of CareWell Clinic's policies and procedures, allowing it to provide accurate and reliable information to patients.

The implementation of WellBot has had a significant impact on CareWell Clinic's operations. The clinic has seen a reduction in administrative costs, improved patient satisfaction, and a decrease in wait times for appointments. WellBot has also freed up the staff to focus on more complex and individualized patient needs. CareWell Clinic's experience highlights the potential of Dify to transform healthcare administration and improve the overall patient experience. They are now exploring using Dify to create personalized health reminders and provide patients with tailored health information based on their individual needs and medical history. The possibilities are truly endless.

These are just a few examples of how Dify is being used to solve real-world business problems and drive tangible results. The platform's versatility and ease of use make it a powerful tool for businesses of all sizes, across a wide range of industries. As you embark on your own AI-powered journey, remember that the key to success is to identify a specific problem, design a targeted solution, and continuously iterate and improve based on user feedback. With Dify, the possibilities are truly limitless.

The Future of No-Code AI: Trends and Predictions

The air crackles with the promise of what's next. We've spent the previous chapters mastering the art of crafting AI-powered solutions without diving into the deep end of code. We've built chatbots, automated workflows, and maybe even started seeing those sweet monetization numbers climb. But the world of AI, especially the no-code corner of it, isn't static. It's a rapidly evolving ecosystem, a digital rainforest teeming with new growth and surprising adaptations. To truly succeed, we need to gaze into the crystal ball (or, perhaps more accurately, analyze the market signals) and anticipate the trends that will shape the future of no-code AI. This chapter isn't about predicting the exact date robots will take over the world (spoiler alert: probably not anytime soon). Instead, it's about understanding the trajectory of no-code AI, identifying emerging technologies, and equipping you with the knowledge to stay ahead of the curve.

The Rise of Hyper-Personalization: AI That Knows You (Really Well)

Remember the days of generic marketing blasts and one-size-fits-all customer service? Thankfully, those days are fading fast. Consumers are demanding experiences tailored to their individual needs and preferences. And AI, particularly when harnessed through no-code platforms, is perfectly positioned to deliver.

Imagine a chatbot that doesn't just answer frequently asked questions but anticipates them based on a user's browsing history, past interactions, and even their expressed sentiment. Think of automated workflows that dynamically adjust based on a customer's purchase behavior, offering personalized recommendations and exclusive deals. This level of hyper-personalization is no longer a futuristic fantasy; it's becoming an expectation.

No-code platforms are democratizing access to the tools needed to achieve this level of personalization. Instead of relying on expensive and time-consuming custom development, businesses can leverage pre-built AI models and intuitive interfaces to create highly personalized experiences. For example, you might integrate your Dify AI chatbot with a CRM system to access customer data and tailor conversations accordingly. You could use sentiment analysis models to identify customers who are feeling frustrated and proactively offer assistance.

The key here is data. The more data you can collect and analyze (ethically and with respect for privacy, of course!), the better you can understand your customers and personalize their experiences. No-code AI platforms are increasingly offering integrations with various data sources, making it easier than ever to gather and utilize this information.

However, beware of the "creepy line." There's a delicate balance between personalization and privacy. Customers appreciate tailored experiences, but they also value their privacy. Be transparent about how you're using their data and give them control over their preferences. Overstepping this boundary can lead to mistrust and damage your brand reputation.

The Convergence of AI and Low-Code: Bridging the Gap

While we've been champions of the no-code revolution, it's important to acknowledge the power of its close cousin: low-code development. Low-code platforms offer a middle ground between no-code's visual simplicity and traditional coding's flexibility. And the future likely holds a convergence of these two approaches.

Think of it this way: No-code platforms are excellent for building standard AI applications and automating common tasks. But what happens when you need to go beyond the pre-built functionalities? What if you need to integrate a highly specialized AI model or create a custom data pipeline? This is where low-code comes in.

Low-code platforms allow you to extend the capabilities of no-code tools by adding custom code snippets or integrating with external APIs. This provides a level of flexibility that is simply not possible with pure no-code solutions. Imagine using a no-code platform to build the core functionality of your chatbot and then using a low-code extension to integrate a custom AI model for sentiment analysis that you trained yourself.

This convergence of no-code and low-code is particularly exciting for businesses that want to rapidly prototype and deploy AI solutions without sacrificing the ability to customize and scale. It allows them to leverage the speed and ease of use of no-code while retaining the power and flexibility of low-code.

The key is to find platforms that seamlessly integrate no-code and low-code capabilities. Look for platforms that offer visual interfaces for building AI applications but also allow you to add custom code or integrate with external APIs when needed. This will give you the best of both worlds.

The Democratization of AI Model Training: Everyone Can Be an AI Expert

One of the biggest barriers to entry in the world of AI has always been the complexity of training AI models. It used to require deep expertise in machine learning, data science, and programming. But thanks to advancements in no-code AI, this is rapidly changing.

We're seeing the emergence of no-code platforms that allow you to train your own AI models without writing a single line of code. These platforms typically provide intuitive interfaces for uploading data, selecting model architectures, and training the models. They also automate many of the complex tasks involved in model training, such as data preprocessing, feature engineering, and hyperparameter tuning.

This democratization of AI model training has profound implications. It means that anyone, regardless of their technical background, can build and deploy custom AI models that are tailored to their specific needs. For example, a marketing manager could train an AI model to predict which leads are most likely to convert. A customer service representative could train an AI model to identify and resolve common customer issues.

However, it's important to remember that training AI models requires data. The more data you have, the better your models will perform. It's also crucial to ensure that your data is clean, accurate, and representative of the real world. Garbage in, garbage out, as they say.

Furthermore, while these platforms simplify the process of training AI models, it's still important to understand the basics of machine learning. You need to understand the different types of models, their strengths and weaknesses, and how to evaluate their performance. Thankfully, many no-code platforms provide educational resources and tutorials to help you learn these concepts.

The Rise of Edge AI: Bringing Intelligence Closer to the User

Traditionally, AI models have been deployed in the cloud. This means that data is sent from devices to the cloud for processing, and the results are sent back to the devices. However, this approach can be slow, expensive, and unreliable, especially in situations where network connectivity is limited or unavailable.

Edge AI, on the other hand, brings AI processing closer to the user. It involves deploying AI models directly on devices, such as smartphones, tablets, and IoT devices. This allows for faster response times, reduced latency, and improved privacy, as data is processed locally rather than being sent to the cloud.

No-code platforms are playing a key role in the rise of edge AI. They provide tools for building and deploying AI models that are optimized for edge devices. These tools often include features such as model compression, quantization, and hardware acceleration.

The implications of edge AI are vast. Imagine a smart home system that can recognize your face and automatically adjust the lighting and temperature to your preferences, all without sending any data to the cloud. Think of a manufacturing plant that can use AI to detect defects in real-time, preventing costly errors and improving product quality.

However, edge AI also presents some challenges. Edge devices typically have limited processing power and memory, which means that AI models need to be highly optimized to run efficiently. It's also important to consider the security of edge devices, as they are often more vulnerable to attack than cloud servers.

The Ethical Considerations: Building Responsible AI

As AI becomes more powerful and pervasive, it's crucial to consider the ethical implications of its use. AI can be used for good, but it can also be used for harm. It's important to ensure that AI is used responsibly and ethically.

No-code platforms can play a role in promoting ethical AI development. They can provide tools for detecting and mitigating bias in AI models. They can also help to ensure that AI systems are transparent and explainable.

Bias in AI models can arise from biased data or biased algorithms. If an AI model is trained on biased data, it will likely produce biased results. For example, if an AI model is trained to predict loan defaults using data that is biased against certain demographic groups, it will likely discriminate against those groups.

Transparency and explainability are also crucial for ethical AI. It's important to understand how AI systems make decisions so that we can identify and correct any errors or biases. Explainable AI (XAI) techniques can help to make AI systems more transparent and understandable.

As the power of AI continues to grow, so too does the responsibility for its ethical deployment. By embracing ethical considerations from the outset and leveraging the tools available within no-code platforms, we can ensure that AI is used to create a more just and equitable future for all.